MW00938721

ms. Wendy
Thanks for your
Support!
Mr. Adrienne   9-21-13

AW
"2018"
Thnx Jan
for your support.

# How My Daughter is a Survivor of Sickle Cell Disease

ADRIENNE F. EASTER

authorHOUSE®

*AuthorHouse*™
*1663 Liberty Drive*
*Bloomington, IN 47403*
*www.authorhouse.com*
*Phone: 1-800-839-8640*

*First published by AuthorHouse 6/10/2010*

*ISBN: 978-1-4343-7451-6 (sc)*

*Library of Congress Control Number: 2010908578*

*Printed in the United States of America*
*Bloomington, Indiana*

*This book is printed on acid-free paper.*

## *My Special Thanks*

Avonna Williams: my daughter

Ken Best: my son

Jude Best: my husband

To my entire family:
the Easters, Robinsons, Coopers,
and
Williams

# Contents

# CHAPTER 1

# The Beginning: A Mother's Worst Nightmare

On November 10, 1985, a baby girl was born to me and Myron Williams. This girl was discovered to have sickle-cell anemia (sickle-cell disease type SS). We, as young, new parents at the ages of twenty-five and thirty, did not know anything about this disease. I was in trouble and didn't know what to do. My baby was still in the hospital, and I was at home. I received a phone call from Kaiser Hospital on November 14, 1985, about my daughter having sickle-cell anemia. I began to cry; I couldn't believe it. Then I began to scream, "Why me?" and I asked the nurse on the phone if she was sure. "You must have the wrong child! Or you have made a mistake!"

I took Avonna to Children's Hospital for a second opinion. After we had the lab work done, we waited in the waiting room for the results. I was so nervous that I was pacing the floor with Avonna in my arms. I started to bite my nails. It seemed like it took forever for them to call my name. Finally, the lab technician called my name, we went into a room, and he told me to have a seat. Once I sat down, he told me to try to relax—but the news he had for me wasn't what I wanted to hear. It was true: Avonna's results showed that she had sickle-cell anemia. I didn't want the results to be positive for sickle-cell; I didn't even know what that was! I had to make an appointment with the genetic counselor at Kaiser Hospital for the information that I would need. The counselor sat down and began to tell me about how a person gets sickle-cell anemia, which, it turns out, all starts with the parents having traits of the disease.

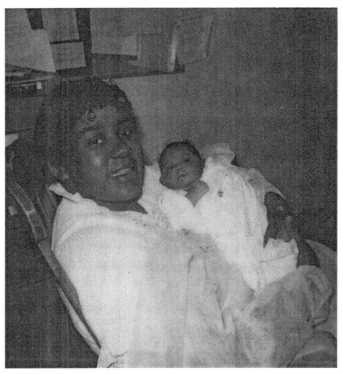

Me (Mom) holding Avonna as a
baby. Avonna was 4 days old.

# CHAPTER 2

## *Avonna's Childhood*

I got the trait from my mother, who didn't even know she had it until 2003, when she was tested. I feel that every African American should be tested for sickle-cell anemia to be safe. The genetic counselors with whom I met showed me how Avonna was born with sickle-cell anemia: a trait of S was taken from me, and a trait of S was taken from her father. I learned that there are three different types of sickle-cell disease: SA, SC, and SS. SA and SC are mainly in the jointed areas in the body, with SS being the worst type, due to its presence in the spleen, which is what produces the blood and makes it flow into the stomach and the rest of the body. This worst type is what Avonna ended up being diagnosed with.

I was extremely upset, of course, because I didn't know what to expect. I began to ask questions and seek help and support with how to learn about the disease.

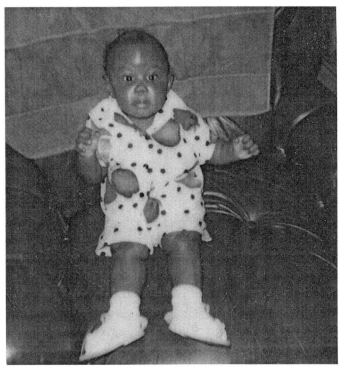

Avonna 6 months old.

# CHAPTER 3

## Blood Transfusions

My first question that I had was "What signs should I look for when my child is in pain, because a child is going to cry *anyway?*" The genetic counselor told me that I would have to pay close attention to my child. So I was very observant and very protective of her. Avonna didn't cry unless she was hungry or in pain; she was a happy and playful baby. As time went on and Avonna grew, she stayed healthy—until, when she was nine months old, her stomach started to swell and get hard. I knew immediately that something was going wrong with my daughter, so I rushed her to Kaiser Hospital in Oakland, California, where the emergency staff began to work on her. Also, I had paged the hematologist to let them know about Avonna. As a parent, I was scared: it was my daughter's first sickle-cell crisis. Avonna had a high fever of 101. Any time a sickle-cell patient has a fever over 101, he or she must be hospitalized and given fluids and antibiotics to get better. As time went on, I started to understand more and more about the disease.

Avonna's next crisis was when she was eleven months old, when she developed pneumonia. That's another thing: when sickle-cell patients get sick from a cold, it gets worse than it normally would because the sickle-cell adversely affects their immune systems. So there I was, back at the hospital again and seeing the same thing: an IV in Avonna's foot as she took fluids and antibiotics.

As time went by, Avonna got better. She was out, doing better, doing fine—and then, two months later, the same ordeal! Avonna was sick again, and all I could think was, *God, why is this happening to me and my child?* I hated to see my Avonna suffer so much, but there was nothing I could do. So she had the same treatments as before, and I realized that I had to get a grip on myself. Mentally and emotionally, I was stressed, but as time went on, I began to learn more and more as I watched my child's behavior and body language. After Avonna got better, she was fine for awhile, doing good for about another two months.

I'm holding Avonna (Mom). Avonna is 1 years old.

# CHAPTER 4

## *Medications & Narcotics*

One morning at about two, Avonna woke up, screaming in pain. I jumped out of bed, very frantic and scared. Avonna's stomach had swelled, as big and as hard as a brick. Where I lived was in the ghetto, so I knocked on the wall of my apartment to get the attention of my next-door neighbor Chester. Chester was always available to help me to get Avonna to the hospital. Back to Oakland's Kaiser I went, but first, I paged the doctors to let them know I was on my way with Avonna. Back then, I still had to go the emergency room, where I would sit for eight to ten hours watching my child suffer. At times, Kaiser's staff acted liked they didn't care. There were times when I felt like suing them over the poor service my daughter received, but once I complained to her doctors, the service got a little better for her.

This went on for a long time. Every two to three months, I was going back and forth to the hospital for the same things over and over again: sickle-cell crisis and blood transfusions. Avonna had her pleasant days—and sometimes *weeks*. But when she turned seven, she was hospitalized for pneumonia. The fluid kept building up in her lungs until she had congestive heart failure. She went into a coma, and the doctors told me that she would not live through the night. I was crying and screaming; I didn't want my child to die! I began to pray. I called all of my family members to let them know what had happened to Avonna; she had never been this sick before. The doctors told me she had to have a "transfusion exchange." I had never heard of such a thing, so I asked the doctors what it was. They took me into a room and sat me down and began to explain the procedure. They also told me that this would be the only thing that could save her life—but it was a fifty-fifty chance. I didn't know what to say, but I had to make a decision. I told the doctors to go ahead and do it.

The procedure was a very long one that took all night. Avonna was hooked up to a lot of machines; she was unconscious and not even breathing on her own. As a parent, I felt helpless and scared, but I tried to be very strong for my baby girl. The doctors had these tubes through which they started drawing Avonna's blood out her body and, at the same time, putting fresh blood in. This was a trip for me to see all that blood coming out and going in, with Avonna being so helpless. This went on all night until the morning, but still nothing had changed.

Avonna as a little girl.

# CHAPTER 5

## *Lab Work / Avonna Sees a Psychiatrist*

By the middle of the week Avonna's eyes had opened. It was a blessing for me just to see my child respond to the nurses and doctors. We all were happy and surprised that Avonna's eyes had opened, and the staff started saying that Avonna was a "miracle baby." I and my family were at peace. As time went by, Avonna got better, and the doctor talked to me about her taking medication. This medication was called Hydroxurea, which was a form of chemotherapy. This medication was very strong, so it had very peculiar side effects: loss of hair, nausea, vomiting, and rash. Although I didn't like the sound of it, this time I didn't have a choice but to go ahead with the treatment; yes, I was afraid, and Avonna was, too, but I was told that if I didn't make this choice, she could die. So we started her on the medication, and Avonna got very sick because the medication was in capsules, and the plastic irritated her stomach. She vomited a lot, and so the next day I opened the capsule, poured the powder on a spoon, and put it in Avonna's mouth. She had juice to take it with it, and it worked out fine.

I called her doctor and discussed the situation with him, and he told me that he would have to get back to me because he didn't know if Avonna was benefiting from the medicine. He finally did and told me that was okay, and Avonna was happy. She was also taking other medications, such as penicillin, folic acid, Flovent and Intal inhalers, and Adbrutel. Avonna, now seven, didn't like taking all these different medications, so I had to watch her take her medicine because she didn't want to take them. But as time went on, Avonna came to understand that, in the end, this was all benefiting her, and she started to get better somewhat.

Avonna

# CHAPTER 6

## *Avonna's Teenage Years*

Every month, Avonna had to get lab work done to make sure her blood counts were okay; but she was terrified of needles, and so whenever it was time for her to get her labs done, she would scream and cry. I decided to take her to see a psychiatrist to get over her fear. Avonna got so good that she would offer her arm *willingly* when she went in for her lab work! This is a lot of stress for a child and a parent, but having Christ in my life helped me out a lot and enabled me to be strong for my child and for myself.

Avonna's episodes started to get a little easier for her, due to the medication, prayer, and church. She would still have episodes of back pain—barely walking—and I would have to take her to Kaiser for antibiotics and morphine. Despite her ordeals, she didn't like to stop being active; sometimes, too, she would be rebellious about taking her medicine every day. This was hard for her and me, and I had to really work to convince Avonna to limit her activity.

As time went on, she started to adjust to this system, but then, once again, she had another sickle-cell crisis and became so sick that the Make-A-Wish Foundation granted her wish to meet Michael Jackson! They flew us to Los Angeles, and her wish was granted. Avonna was so excited and happy, and I was, too—this was a great experience for me as a parent.

Avonna's health fluctuated. Finally, after being back in school and doing fine for a while, suddenly Avonna got really sick again. She couldn't finish school and had to have a teacher come to our home to teach her, and she was able to pass for the next year.

Avonna

# Chapter 7

## Avonna Starts High School

Finally, Avonna had started doing better. Now, it was getting closer to her ninth birthday, and we were getting ready to celebrate this big day on November 10, 1994. Avonna was very excited, and I was too. Avonna's favorite character was Ariel from *The Little Mermaid*, so we had a theme party and invited a lot of Avonna's friends and family members. Avonna made it through this day without any pain crisis.

Four years later, Avonna had survived through four more years of pain and blood transfusions. Now she was turning thirteen—a teenager—so I had a great big celebration for Avonna, also celebrating my thirty-eighth birthday alongside her. Avonna was so happy, and all of her school friends and our family came. My co-workers also came, and this was nice. But then, after the party, Avonna started to get sick again; she had another pain crisis, so it was back to Kaiser for morphine, fluids, and another blood transfusion. Avonna was in the hospital for a few days.

That year was very difficult for Avonna, being a teen and with the pressure at school. She was in junior high, and the teachers didn't want to believe that she was sick. I had to call a meeting with them to tell them about her sickle-cell anemia. I had it hard as a parent explaining her illness to the teachers, especially when they told me, "But she *looks* fine!" I had to underscore that it's not in her looks, but inside her body.

Avonna turned fourteen and began high school. This was a big day for her, and she was nervous and scared, but she did it. The years went by, and soon enough Avonna was to be graduating; this was the *big* day of June 12, 2003. Her grandparents came down from Seattle for her ceremony, and I threw Avonna a big party with all of her friends, cousins, aunts and uncles, and other grandparents, and it was beautiful and fun. The party ended about midnight, and Avonna was very tired. She rested well, but resting wasn't enough for her. The next day, she had a really bad crisis had to go to the clinic at Kaiser for fluids, an IV, and morphine. We were there all day until that evening, and Avonna had to continue Vicodin for several days until the pain went away.

Avonna at home on her birthday.

# CHAPTER 8

## *Avonna Starts College*

Finally, Avonna was ready to register for college; she wanted to be a medical assistant. She went and registered for her classes and began attending Contra Costa College. As time went by, Avonna kept getting sick; she was in and out of the hospital until her doctor said no more school. So Avonna had to withdraw from all her classes because her health had started to fail her; she was very sick, and this wasn't good. By this time, we had moved to Vallejo, California, so Avonna and I had to adjust to her new doctor and to a new hospital. We adjusted very well and quickly and were very pleased. The doctor was very good and very concerned about her health. She put Avonna on a transfusion program where Avonna is getting blood every thirty days to keep her out of the hospital. This plan had been working for Avonna. On January 1, 2004, when Avonna was eighteen, we went to a New Year's celebration at my friend Dorothy's house to celebrate with her and her family and friends. Avonna was doing fine. But the next day, Avonna took ill—very ill; she began to breathe very shallowly, and she began to fall down so much that she couldn't walk.

I called 911 for help as my daughter's eyes began to roll back into her head. Avonna was dying. I was going crazy, screaming "Hold on baby; please don't die yet!" The paramedics got there and began to work on her. They got her back to stable condition, and then they took her to Kaiser, where they continued to work on her. As a parent, I had never experienced this before in life. I was shaken and stunned, asking the doctors what was going on. In her eighteen years, the disease had never affected her this way. The doctor explained to me that this could happen because her oxygen could be shut off from her cells, so we needed to be aware from now on of this phase of sickle-cell anemia. Avonna was so sick that she was in the hospital for almost two weeks; she had to have three units of blood to bounce back.

As she started recovering, she asked me what had happened, because she couldn't remember. But then, three weeks later, she said to me, "Mom, I was dying! I felt my oxygen leaving my body, that's why I had made peace inside with you and my brother. But I myself began to call out to God in my mind, and I asked God: 'Help me! Don't let me die! I want to live!' God answered my prayer."

Avonna at home.

# CHAPTER 9

## Avonna's Adulthood

On April 11, 2005, Avonna fell victim again. This time, though, it was even worse—her breathing had completely stopped. I had to do CPR on my own daughter until paramedics got there! This experience was hard for me; I had never done CPR on anybody. This took a lot out of me—but God knows how much you can bear.

Avonna's doctor talked to us about Avonna having blood transfusions every 5 weeks and Avonna having to start a treatment called Deferoxamine infusion. This treatment helps prevent the iron buildup in the body that results from receiving so many transfusions. This procedure was scary because I had to learn how to inject a needle into Avonna's arm or stomach every night. We went to the transfusion clinic in Vallejo, where the nurses showed me how to do this procedure. I was nervous, and so I messed up and had to start over—but the second time around, I got it.

The medicine was delivered to our house, and we started the procedure. The first step is to wash your hands; then you sterilize the skin area; then you stick the needle into the sterilized area, which could be on the arm or the stomach. Avonna does not like going through this, but she knows it has to be done. We have been doing this procedure now for two years, and Avonna's iron count has been cut in half, which is a good thing because Avonna is getting blood transfusions every five weeks. This procedure will be done for the rest of her life. The blood transfusions are really helping Avonna so far. The last time Avonna was in the hospital before now was February 2006. I am happy that Avonna is doing a lot better; the only thing is that when she gets blood transfusions, her face swells up. Some days are good and some not so good, and her personality changes at times, but life isn't perfect. We will be battling this disease for the rest of Avonna's life. Maybe, one day, Avonna will find a match for a bone marrow transplant, even though that would be a big risk—a fifty-fifty chance on her life. But through it all and despite it all, God is good, and I know He is the One keeping my daughter alive—and I give all of my glory to Him!

A picture of me (Mom).

# CHAPTER 10

# Avonna's Appointment at the Infusion Clinic

September 29, 2007, was not a good day for Avonna. This was the day for a blood transfusion at 9:00 AM. We arrived and were told that something had gone wrong with the blood and that the lab was screening more blood for Avonna. At 10:45, we were still waiting for the blood, so the receptionist went to go check to see what was going on. In the meantime, the nurses had forgotten about Avonna. They had forgotten to do her vital signs and to get her IV started for her blood transfusion! Finally, the receptionist arrived back with the blood, but Avonna veins were not cooperating with the nurses. Three different nurses had tried for her veins in both arms and hands. Avonna had been stuck eleven times in her arms and hands, and the veins just had clotted; they couldn't get a vein for Avonna's blood transfusion. This was a great disappointment for me, but more so for Avonna.

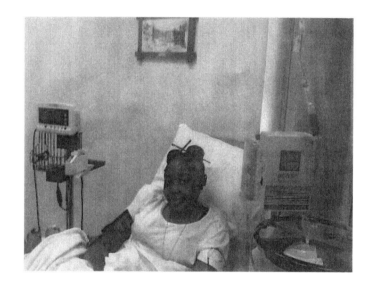

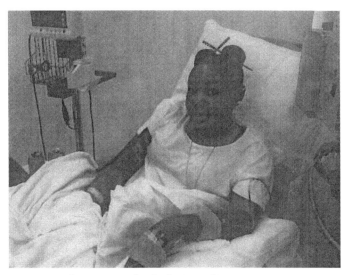

Avonna at the Infusion clinic getting
her iv for blood transfusion.

# CHAPTER 11

## How I Feel about Having Sickle-Cell Anemia Disease at the Age of Twenty-Two

When I was old enough to realize and understand that I had sickle-cell anemia, I was five years old. When I was younger than that, I really didn't understand that I had it because I was still in my baby stages. Growing up having sickle-cell anemia wasn't easy, because as a child, I wasn't able to do many activities that normal children were able to do. I didn't understand why I couldn't run around and play as much as I wanted to, and I remember my mom used to always tell me, "Avonna, you need to sit down and take a break" or "Avonna, don't overdo it!" and I used to cry and get upset because I wanted to do normal activities like other normal children—but I simply *couldn't*.

As I got older leading up to my teen years, I fully understood that I had sickle-cell anemia, and I knew what I could and couldn't do. I remember suffering so much that my doctor put me on this medication called Hydroxuria, which was a capsule form of chemo for cancer patients. There were a lot of side effects to this medication, including vomiting and hair loss. This was a big struggle for me because, for one, I simply didn't want to take it, and also, I was afraid of the side effects. At this time, though, I had no choice, because I was suffering so much I almost died. My doctor told my mom and me that this was our last option. Taking this medication was a struggle for me, because my stomach was irritating by the capsules. As time went by, I started to lose my hair. This began happening in the beginning of my teen years. I was fourteen years old when the situation with my hair got worse, and I was forced to cut it. This was a very hard decision for me to make. I had two options: the first one was to keep taking the medication and let my hair continue to fall out; my second option was to continue taking this medication and cut my hair so that I wouldn't lose it completely.

Finally, my teenage years were here, which meant high school, peers, guys, and—most of all—*dating*. In high school, I had friends, but they didn't know about my illness; I was afraid of what people might think or say about me. But eventually, I did tell my friends, and they were very understanding and nonjudgmental. That meant a lot to me to have friends that understood my situation. I was also starting to get interested in guys and dating. Liking guys and dating wasn't easy, though, because whenever I liked a guy (or if he was my boyfriend), I would tell him about my sickle-cell—which I felt that he should know about so that in the case of a sickle-cell crisis, the guy would be aware of what to do. But when

I was comfortable enough to tell the guy, his reaction was always very rude, negative, and, most of all, hurtful. These guys would say things such as, "You're contagious," "I can't be with someone who is sick," and "You're not healthy." Or else I just wouldn't even hear from them again. That was very hard for me to deal with, but in spite of all the negativity, peers, and high school, I made it and am a better person for it.

I graduated high school and decided that I wanted to go to college to become a medical assistant; now I was reaching adulthood. Going to college was okay at first. I was working and going to school, but it soon became too stressful, and I got really sick—so sick that my doctor took me out of school and stopped me from working. That was mentally and emotionally stressful for me, because I wanted to work and go to school like everyone else; but I just had to take it one day at a time and rest and get better.

At that time, I had a boyfriend, but our relationship didn't work out. Now, though, as an adult of twenty-two years of age, I'm very happy with my life. I finally found the love of my life. His name is D'quan Nelson. I'm very happy with our relationship. D'quan knows everything about my sickle-cell, and he is very caring, understanding, and, most of all, supportive. It has been a very long road for me; these twenty-two years have been rough, but in spite of all the pain and suffering, I'm so grateful to God that I'm that I'm still here! If it wasn't for Jesus Christ, I could have been dead a long time ago. Also, if it wasn't for my wonderful mother, I don't know where I would be or what I would be doing. My mom is my everything, and I love her with all my heart.

Being twenty-two and having sickle-cell anemia isn't always easy. To this day, I still have my episodes of having sickle-Cell crises, but they're not bad to the point where I have to go to the hospital and get an IV. I can maintain the pain at home by taking Vicodin and morphine. I have not been in the hospital for two years now. I'm doing very well. What has been keeping me well is that I get blood transfusions every six weeks. Getting blood transfusions isn't always easy, though, because it has different side effects, such as swelling in the face, allergic reactions, and the body's rejection of the blood. In the last two years, I have experienced some of these symptoms. In spite of all I have been through, though, I can say,

"You can be a survivor of sickle cell anemia!"

Avonna and her boyfriend.

# CHAPTER 12

## *Guiding Children, Teens, and Adults through Life with Sickle-Cell Anemia*

Parents need to care for their children's health; parents also need to focus on their children's needs. When children with sickle-cell start going to school, they are beginning a new stage in their life. Your children will be spending a lot of time away from you and in the care of other adults. Children with sickle-cell anemia will also be spending time with other children their own ages. Your children's social and school lives may create new questions and problems. For you parents, this would be a perfect time to teach your children how to learn how to do things for themselves.

Avonna and her doctor.

# CHAPTER 13

## *Parents of Sickle-Cell Patients Should Let Their Children Do Things for Themselves*

Children with sickle-cell anemia can learn how to care of themselves even though they have this illness. Your children need to do things on their own, but as their parents, you still have to make sure that your children are getting what they need. Sometimes your children may not ask to do certain things on their own, and as a parent, you may need to push them a little. Sometimes we parents may feel guilty or afraid, but we shouldn't let our children's illness get in the way of helping them grow up. It's okay to let our children fail and make mistakes, because this is part of how we learn about what we can do. Don't always do everything for your children, because when you let them do things on their own, they feel good about themselves. As parents, it's also okay to protect your children because they have an illness.

Mom and Dad.

# Chapter 14

## *Talking About Self-Esteem Issues while Having Sickle-Cell Anemia*

Parents of sickle-cell patients, you should help your children feel good about themselves. You should help them, notice their skills and strengths, and pay attention to some things your children are interested in. You should praise your children when they have done something very well. You should show your children that you are listening to what they have to say; by listening to them, you show them that you care about what they think and how they feel. You could also help your children get involved in different activities. You need to teach your children to accept themselves even though they have sickle-cell anemia. As humans, we all like to feel good about ourselves and like we belong. Children with sickle-cell may be afraid that they won't fit in, because having this illness would make them feel like they're different, and they also may think that other children and people will make fun of them for this. Some children may feel good about telling their friends about their sickle-cell anemia, but others won't want anyone to know. When their friends *do* know about their illness, though, they can have the benefit of peer support. If your children don't know how to tell their friends, you should let them practice with you first. One your children have told their friends about the illness, they should feel better about themselves.

Avonna with Mom and brother.

# CHAPTER 15

## Teaching Your Children How to Succeed in School While Having Sickle-Cell Anemia

Most children want to do well in school. Doing well in school builds a strong future. Parents, you should be partners with your children's teachers. When it is a new school year, you should go to the school and meet your child's teacher and the school nurse; and when you go to meet with them, you should bring your child with you so that he or she can ask any questions that he or she may have. You should tell the teacher about sickle-cell and give him or her some information to read in order to learn more about the disease. The teacher needs to know that your child may sometimes come to school with minor aches and pains. Your child should be sent home only if he or she has a fever or severe pain—or if he or she otherwise needs to see a doctor. You need to explain to your child their special needs, such as the following:

1. Getting water when he or she is thirsty
2. Going to the bathroom as soon as he or she feels the need to go
3. Making up schoolwork if he or she has to miss school
4. Resting or slowing down if he or she is tired or sore. For example, during gym class, he or she may only be able to run two laps, not six (but most sickle-cell patients will not have to have physical-education class)
5. Rejoining the class as soon as he or she is ready to
6. Getting medicine if he or she needs it

As a parent, you should check to see if your child's teacher is giving your child what is needed. Some teachers may protect your child too much, while other teachers may ignore your child. If you have concerns, you should talk to the teacher. As a parent, you need to stand up for your child's rights, which means that if your child needs extra attention or help, the school needs to give it to him or her. Most important of all, just expect the best for your child, and he or she should do very well.

Avonna

# CHAPTER 16

## *Parents: You Need to Care for Yourself and Your Family*

As a parent, you may do all you can to help your children stay well, but they may still have problems. These problems can affect the whole family. As your child grows up, you may face new issues, such as learning problems and pain. As time goes on, you may feel scared and angry again, even though you may have thought those feelings had gone for good. As a parent, it is very important for you to take care of yourself; you need to learn about your own limits and needs. You may need time to yourself, your other children, and your work. If you have other children, you need to show them attention and that you care about them as well; you should make time to talk to them about what's going on. Try to be involved with their school activities as well; don't just put all your focus on the child that has sickle-cell. You should teach all of your children about sickle-cell disease, because they may have questions and concerns about their brother or sister. In order to have a healthy family, you should treat your child with sickle-cell like his or her brothers and sisters as much as possible: try to use the same system of discipline and reward with all of your children. If you feel alone, you can always ask for help and support for your family.

# CHAPTER 17

# The Teen Years

Parents, your teens can still have many of the same problems that younger children have from sickle-cell. Infections, pain, low blood counts, and strokes can affect people with sickle-cell at any age. Some of these problems are less dangerous for teens, like infections, which can now be treated with pills at home and do not necessitate an IV at the hospital. Parents, your teen will need to see a doctor if he or she has a fever over 101 degrees Fahrenheit. Here are the most common health problems that teens with sickle-cell anemia face:

1. Pain
2. Eye problems
3. Leg ulcers
4. Aseptic necrosis
5. Appearance
6. Infections
7. Gallstones
8. Acute chest syndrome
9. Priapism

# CHAPTER 18

## Sickle-Cell Patients Having Severe Pain

Some teens with Sickle-Cell Disease have more pain as they get older. The pain may feel worse or just come more often. Getting treatment for pain is the same for teens as it is for children. Parents, if your teen has had a lot of problems with pain, he or she has mostly tried to ease the pain; so it makes sense for your teens to use the treatment(s) that work the best for them.

Dehydration (lack of fluid in the body) is a common trigger for pain at this age. Most teens get involved in sports and other activities, and they don't take the time to stop and drink fluids or take a break to rest. Teens that have sickle-cell need to find ways to take care of themselves, since you can't always be there to remind them of what they need to do in order to stay healthy. Some teenage girls get severe menstrual pain that brings on a sickle-cell crisis. The doctor may be able to prescribe a hormone to prevent this severe pain. Parents, your teens will learn more about what triggers their pain as they do new things; you should suggest that they watch to see what happens with the pain. If your teen finds something that often leads to pain, he or she can stay away from it or take very special care with it. For teens with chronic pain, a "pain contract" is an agreement about how pain will be handled. These contracts are often used in hospitals but can also be helpful at home. Pain contracts have two parts: the first part says what the health care staff will do to help the teen manage his or her pain; the second part states what the teen will do for him- or herself to manage the pain.

(Note to parents: If your teen has a fever with pain, or if he or she has pain in the chest or stomach, he or she should be seen by a doctor *right away.* Call first so that your teen can be seen as soon as possible.

## CHAPTER 19

# Sickle-Cell Patients Have a Different Appearance Than "Normal" People

Some teens that have sickle-cell will have late puberty. They reach puberty about two years later than others their age. Puberty means many changes. These changes are the same for teens with and without sickle-cell; the only difference is *when* puberty happens.

For the teen girls, puberty is when their breasts grow and their periods start. For teen boys, their facial hair grows, their muscles get bigger, and their voices deepen. Puberty also means being able to get—or to make someone—pregnant. Having late puberty is not a problem in itself, but it can make your teen feel anxiety and embarrassment. If your teen is feeling concern about these issues, talk to the doctor.

Some teens that have sickle-cell may be small and thin for their age. Children with sickle-cell catch up late in their teen years. People that have sickle-cell can also have yellow eyes from time to time, which is caused by a yellow substance called bilirubin that comes from broken-down red-blood cells. In some people, the yellow tint lasts for a long time—or it may *always* be there. This issue is not a medical problem, unless the eyes become much more yellow than they were before. If that happens, contact your teen's doctor.

# CHAPTER 20

## *Living with Your Teen Who Has Sickle-Cell*

The teen years are a time of major changes for you and your teen. There is a lot you can do to help your teen during these times. There are also a lot of things that you will not have any control over. As a parents, your support and help will still matter, but at the same time, your teens will be making their own choices in their lives. Your teens will learn how take care of themselves during these years. They will also be getting ready for the time when they will be on their own. Your teens are growing up; although they will need limits, they will also need freedom At the same time, your teens will keep trying to find their own balance that works well for them.

# CHAPTER 21

## *Parents: You Should Let Your Teens with Sickle-Cell Do Things for Themselves*

Before you know it, your teen will be an adult and living on his or her own. As parents, you should start helping your teens have control over their lives. Teens that have sickle-cell often feel chained to the disease; they also feel angry: they have to listen to a lot of adults, and they feel like they should be doing things on their own because they want to be independent as teens. Parents, your teens may not take as good care of themselves as they should, you should let them try anyway. Talk to them about their illness so that they can know how to do things for themselves. You need to trust your teens to ask for help when they need it, and whenever they make a mistake, help them learn from it. If your teens learn now, they can take control of their lives as adults.

There are so many ways for your teen to be independent, such as their clothing styles, musical preferences, and even the way they do their hair. As parents, you may not like the way your teens present themselves or act, but you should still accept them, unless they are bringing endangerment or doing harm to themselves or others. Growing up as a teen and having sickle-cell can be scary; try to get your teens involved in different activities, instead of letting them focus on their disease. These activities, such as hobbies, clubs, part-time jobs, or sports, will give your teens the chance to be with others and prepare for the future.

# CHAPTER 22

## *Parents: Set Limits for Your Teens*

Parents, you are in charge! You have the right to know what your teens are doing and whom they are hanging out with. It is your job to decide how much freedom to allow. Setting these limits should protect your teens and should concern curfew, homework, chores, and, if applicable, the use of a car. You should discuss these rules with your teens and make sure that these limits are clear to the both of you. If your teens decide to break the rules that you have set for them, it's okay to respond with proportionate consequences; having sickle-cell is *not* an excuse for them to break your rules. Like other teens, young people with sickle-cell sometimes take risks. Teens feel that they have a need to fit in with their friends, and drugs, alcohol, and sex are some things that teens get involved with in order to prove themselves. Teens with sickle-cell, however, may have a stronger need to prove that they can fit in with other teens. Here are some dangerous risks for your teen with Sickle cell:

1. Sex without condoms, which bring a greater risk of getting a sexually transmitted disease (STD).

2. Getting pregnant, which can be more of a risk for your teen.

3. Alcohol, which can increase sickling because it dehydrates the body.

4. Cigarettes, which can also increase sickling because smoke lowers the oxygen level in the blood.

All these are risks for any teen, but they can cause *more* harm to teens with sickle-cell. Parents, if your teens are taking risks, you need to get involved. Your teens also need your guidance and support, as their parents, to show them that you care.

# Chapter 23

# Parents: Build Your Teenagers' Self-Esteem

Like all teenagers, teens that have sickle-cell anemia may have low self-esteem. As parents, there are many things you can do to make your teens feel good about themselves, such as:

1. Listen to what your teens have to tell you.
2. Don't put your teens down.
3. Encourage your teens.
4. Do different activities with your teens.
5. Help your teens feel better about their bodies.
6. Let your teens know how good you feel about being their parents.

Parents, your teens need to feel like you are listening to them when they are talking to you. Even if you don't like what they have to tell you, you still should listen, because that will show them that you care about them. If you are not sure about what your teens mean or how they feel, make sure you ask them questions. No matter what the situation is, don't put your teens down, because if you do, it will make them feel bad about themselves. If your teens have done something that you don't like, you should sit them down and tell them how the situation affected you. Your teens need your respect and praise.

You need to do different activities with your teens, even if sometimes you don't want to. Try to find things that you both may like. It could be going to the movies, playing basketball, or attending a concert. Teens that have sickle-cell anemia often feel ashamed of their bodies. Some look younger than their friends because they mature late; some feel embarrassed by their appearance because they have scars from IVs.

You should let your teens know that you feel good about them being your children. Also, you should encourage your teens with things that they may want to do. Make sure you ask your teens about school, work, or any special projects. Showing them that you are paying attention will show them that you believe that what they do has value.

# Chapter 24

# Make Plans for the Future and for School

Many teens that have sickle-cell anemia miss a lot of school. Some teens may have manage to still do well in school, but others have major problems such as falling behind and developing poor study habits. Parents, your teens may feel depressed about the future; as parents, you have to encourage your teens to do very well in school. If your teens have missed a lot school, you can arrange make-up school for them. When they reach high school, it is time for them to really focus on their schoolwork and their future after high school. Parents, your teens will now have to decide if they are going to want to go to college. Many people with sickle-cell do go, but if they have a lot of problems with their illness, they may have to finish school later and take care of their health first. Encourage your teens to plan for a full life and a future. Teens that have sickle-cell worry about finding a job; they are afraid that they won't be able to support themselves. Parents, support your teens! Tell them that people who have sickle-cell can be successful!

# CHAPTER 25

## *The Adult Years: For Adults Who Have Sickle-Cell Anemia*

Working and having a family are the main issues of adulthood for those who have sickle-cell. Adults that have sickle-cell *can* manage to have full lives. Many are able to live on their own and have job and take care of their homes and their children. Adults *can* enjoy life while having sickle-cell anemia. As parents, you can teach your adult children to become independent and happy despite the obstacles they have been faced with their entire lives.

CPSIA information can be obtained at www.ICGtesting.com
Printed in the USA
BVOW001500170513

321026BV00001B/24/P

9 781434 374516